AN **INSIDER'S GUIDE** TO
ALL THE TEAMS IN THE NFL!

TEAM TRACKER

NFL

by JOE LAYDEN

SCHOLASTIC INC.

New York   Toronto   London   Auckland   Sydney
Mexico City   New Delhi   Hong Kong   Buenos Aires

No part of this work may be reproduced in whole or in part, or stored in a retrieval system, or transmitted in any form or by any means, electronic, mechanical, photocopying, recording, or otherwise, without written permission of the publisher. For information regarding permission, write to Scholastic Inc., Attention: Permissions Department, 557 Broadway, New York, NY 10012.

ISBN 0-439-78434-4

Published by Scholastic Inc.
SCHOLASTIC and associated logos are trademarks and/or registered trademarks of Scholastic Inc.

12 11 10 9 8 7 6 5 4 3 2 1   5 6 7 8 9/0

Designed by Michael Malone
Printed in the U.S.A.
First printing, August 2005

ARE YOU READY FOR SOME FOOTBALL?

IT'S TIME FOR ANOTHER ACTION-PACKED NFL SEASON.

And if history tells us anything it's simply this: expect the unexpected. That's half the fun, isn't it? Making predictions and then watching the season unfold. This book will give you a glimpse into the year ahead. It's a glance at each of the league's 32 teams, complete with stats, trivia, and analysis. Consider it a handbook for the 2005 season. There's even a wipe-away standings chart and NFL Playoffs tracking grid to help you follow the action right up to Super Bowl XL!

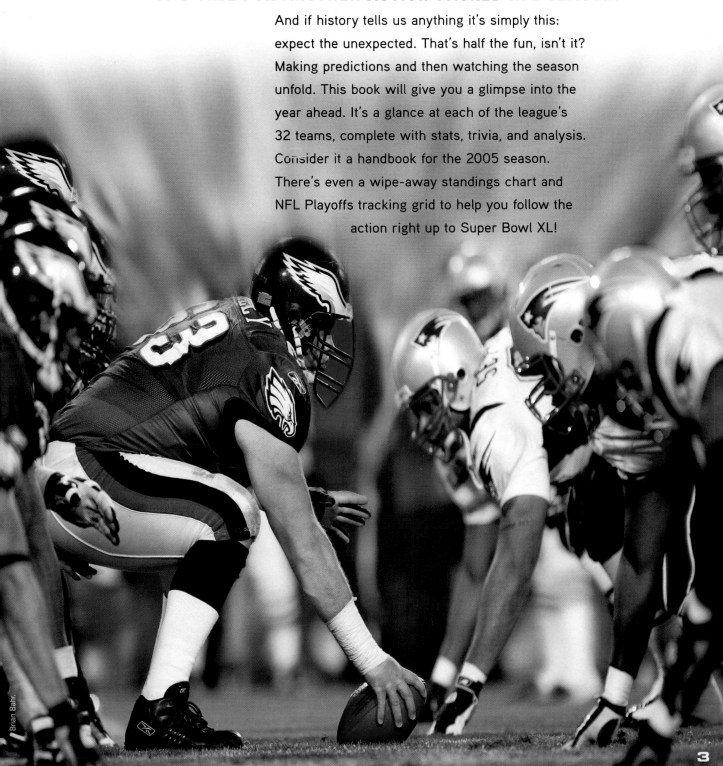

Brian Bahr.

2004 LEADERS

PASSING
Drew Bledsoe
2,932 yards
20 TDs
56.9 comp
76.6 rating

RUSHING
Willis McGahee
1,128 yards

RECEIVING
Eric Moulds
88 receptions
1,043 yards

TACKLES
London Fletcher
92

SACKS
Aaron Schobel
8.0

INTERCEPTIONS
Nate Clements
6

BY THE NUMBERS:

110

That is the number of consecutive games in which Eric Moulds has recorded a catch. It is the longest streak in Bills history.

BUFFALO BILLS

2004 RECORD: **9–7**

The Bills opened the 2004 season slowly, losing four of their first five games. Over the second half of the season, however, they were one of the hottest teams in the NFL, winning eight of their last nine. One of the primary reasons for that resurgence was the outstanding play of running back Willis McGahee. Now fully recovered from a knee injury, Willis cracked the 1,000-yard barrier in rushing. He also scored 13 touchdowns, the second-highest total in Bills history. Opponents will have to focus on Willis in 2005, which should take some of the heat off of promising quarterback J.P. Losman, who steps into a starting role.

Main: Rick Stewart. Inset: Rick Stewart.

* WITH AN UNCANNY KNACK FOR FINDING OPEN SPACE, RUNNING BACK WILLIS McGAHEE HAS EMERGED AS THE STAR OF THE BUFFALO OFFENSE.

2004 TEAM STATS

	RANK	YPG	RUSH YPG	PASS YPG	PTS	PTS/GAME
OFFENSE	25	293.2	117.1	176.1	395	24.7
DEFENSE	2	264.3	100.3	164.0	284	17.8

MIAMI DOLPHINS

2004 RECORD: 4-12

There's no question that 2005 will be a rebuilding year for the Dolphins. Fortunately for new head coach Nick Saban, the Dolphins are not without talent. At the core of the offense is Randy McMichael, who caught 73 passes for 791 yards, setting a single-season team record for receptions by a tight end. McMichael's efforts did not go unnoticed: he was named to the Pro Bowl in only his third season in the league. Led by defensive end Jason Taylor and linebacker Zach Thomas, the Dolphins ranked eighth in the NFL in total defense.

Main: Eliot J. Schecter. Inset: Andy Lyons.

* PRO BOWL TIGHT END RANDY McMICHAEL ENTERS HIS FOURTH SEASON AS ONE OF THE BRIGHTEST YOUNG STARS FOR THE DOLPHINS.

2004 LEADERS

PASSING
A.J. Feeley
1,893 yards
11 TDs
53.7 comp
61.7 rating

RUSHING
Sammy Morris
523 yards

RECEIVING
Chris Chambers
69 receptions
898 yards

TACKLES
Zach Thomas
85

SACKS
Jason Taylor
9.5

INTERCEPTIONS
Arturo Freeman
Sammy Knight
Patrick Surtain
4

BY THE NUMBERS:
305.9

This is the number of yards per game allowed by the Dolphins. The team's defense was ranked No. 8 in the NFL.

2004 TEAM STATS

	RANK	YPG	RUSH YPG	PASS YPG	PTS	PTS/GAME
OFFENSE	29	275.3	83.7	191.6	275	17.2
DEFENSE	8	305.9	143.9	162.0	354	22.1

2004 LEADERS

PASSING
Tom Brady
3,692 yards
28 TDs
60.8 comp
92.6 rating

RUSHING
Corey Dillon
1,635 yards

RECEIVING
David Givens
56 receptions
874 yards

TACKLES
Rodney Harrison
94

SACKS
Willie McGinest
9.5

INTERCEPTIONS
Eugene Wilson
4

BY THE NUMBERS:

92.6

Is this Tom Brady's temperature? No, although he is one cool player. It represents Tom's quarterback rating. Once again, he finished among the NFL leaders in just about every statistical category.

NEW ENGLAND PATRIOTS

2004 RECORD: **14–2**

With their third Super Bowl title in four years, the Patriots officially became a dynasty in 2004. The really scary part? They could be even better in 2005. This is a team that has almost no weaknesses. Let's start at the top, with head coach Bill Belichick, as smart a guy as you will find in the game of football. Belichick made his reputation as a defensive specialist, and there's no question that the Pats are one of the best defensive teams in the league. But they are also strong on offense. Quarterback Tom Brady is a future Hall of Famer. Super Bowl standout Deion Branch is about to become a star at wide receiver. And running back Corey Dillon, picked up in a trade from Cincinnati, was third in the NFL in rushing last season. Anything else we should mention? Oh, yeah, kicker Adam Vinatieri, the hero of two of those Super Bowl victories, has also returned. Bottom line: a fourth Super Bowl trophy is within the Patriots' reach.

* RUNNING BACK COREY DILLON HAS FOUND A HAPPY HOME IN NEW ENGLAND.

Main: Elsa; Inset: Brian Bahr

2004 TEAM STATS

	RANK	YPG	RUSH YPG	PASS YPG	PTS	PTS/GAME
OFFENSE	7	357.6	133.4	224.3	437	27.3
DEFENSE	9	310.8	98.3	212.5	260	16.3

NEW YORK JETS

2004 RECORD: **10–6**

They didn't exactly go from "worst to first," but the New York Jets did a very nice job of turning things around in 2004. After a disappointing 6–10 campaign in 2003, the Jets made some changes on defense and got stand-out performances from their most reliable offensive players. All of which helped the team post a 10–6 record and earn a spot in the playoffs. The team's MVP? No question about it: running back Curtis Martin, a future Hall of Famer whose tenth year in the NFL was easily his finest. Curtis not only led the league in yards gained, but also became the Jets' all-time rushing leader. With Curtis getting stronger each season, and quarterback Chad Pennington continuing to show improvement, the Jets are a team with serious postseason potential in 2005.

Main: Jeff Gross. Inset: Harry How.

* CURTIS MARTIN IS THE JETS' ALL-TIME LEADING RUSHER. NOW HE HAS HIS EYES ON EMMITT SMITH'S NFL RECORD.

2004 LEADERS

PASSING
Chad Pennington
2,673 yards
16 TDs
65.4 comp
91.0 rating

RUSHING
Curtis Martin
1,697 yards

RECEIVING
Santana Moss
45 receptions
838 yards

TACKLES
Jonathan Vilma
77

SACKS
Shaun Ellis
11.0

INTERCEPTIONS
Erik Coleman
4

BY THE NUMBERS:
12
Linebacker Jonathan Vilma was the 12th player taken in the 2004 NFL Draft. So far he hasn't disappointed the Jets or their fans. Jonathan led the Jets in tackles and was named NFL Defensive Rookie of the Year.

2004 TEAM STATS

	RANK	YPG	RUSH YPG	PASS YPG	PTS	PTS/GAME
OFFENSE	12	339.9	149.3	190.6	333	20.8
DEFENSE	7	304.9	97.9	207.0	261	16.3

HOUSTON
2004 RECORD: 7–9
TEXANS

Three years ago, before they'd played a single game, the Houston Texans made a decision that would shape the future of their expansion franchise. They made David Carr their very first draft pick. So far, so good. The gifted 6-3, 230-pound quarterback out of Fresno State has a strong arm and the leadership skills of a much older player. The best news for Texans fans is that David seems only to have skimmed the surface of what he can do. He had his most productive year in 2004, improving in every major statistical category. The Texans have two more All-Pro candidates in wide receiver Andre Johnson and running back Domanick Davis. So don't be surprised if Houston makes some playoff noise in 2005.

2004 LEADERS

PASSING
David Carr
3,531 yards
16 TDs
61.2 comp
83.5 rating

RUSHING
Domanick Davis
1,188 yards

RECEIVING
Andre Johnson
79 receptions
1,142 yards

TACKLES
Jamie Sharper
96

SACKS
Kailee Wong
5.5

INTERCEPTIONS
Dunta Robinson
6

BY THE NUMBERS:
6-3, 219

The height and weight of wide receiver Andre Johnson. Andre, one of the league's best young offensive players, led the Texans in receiving again in 2004.

* DAVID CARR IS STILL ONE OF THE YOUNGEST QUARTER-BACKS IN THE NFL, BUT HE'S PLAYING WITH THE POISE AND POLISH OF A VETERAN. HE HAD HIS BEST SEASON IN 2004.

Main: Jonathan Daniel. Inset: Rick Stewart.

2004 TEAM STATS

	RANK	YPG	RUSH YPG	PASS YPG	PTS	PTS/GAME
OFFENSE	19	320.5	117.6	202.9	309	19.3
DEFENSE	23	341.1	115.2	225.9	339	21.2

INDIANAPOLIS
COLTS

2004 RECORD: **12–4**

Is it possible for Peyton Manning to play any better than he did in 2004? The rest of the NFL certainly hopes the answer to that question is a resounding "No!" Now in his eighth year in a Colts uniform, Peyton is widely regarded as the finest quarterback in the NFL. Before he's through, he'll probably be remembered as one of the best in NFL history. In 2004 he shattered Dan Marino's 20-year-old NFL record for touchdown passes in a single season. That feat, coupled with the fact that he carried the Colts to another AFC South title, helped Peyton earn a second straight MVP award. With an exceptional corps of receivers and a solid running game, the Colts should once again be among the league's most explosive teams. And a Super Bowl title is within their reach.

2004 LEADERS

PASSING
Peyton Manning
4,557 yards
49 TDs
67.6 comp
121.1 rating

RUSHING
Edgerrin James
1,548 yards

RECEIVING
Reggie Wayne
77 receptions
1,210 yards

TACKLES
Cato June
84

SACKS
Dwight Freeney
16.0

INTERCEPTIONS
Jason David
4

Main: Jonathan Daniel. Inset: Rick Stewart.

* WITH THE SPECTACULAR PEYTON MANNING RUNNING THE SHOW AT QUARTERBACK, THE COLTS HAD THE NFL'S HIGHEST-SCORING OFFENSE IN 2004.

BY THE NUMBERS:

16

Sacks registered by defensive end Dwight Freeney. Just in case you think the Colts are strictly an offensive team, there is something you should know: Freeney led the league in this category.

2004 TEAM STATS

	RANK	YPG	RUSH YPG	PASS YPG	PTS	PTS/GAME
OFFENSE	2	404.7	115.8	288.9	522	32.6
DEFENSE	29	370.6	127.3	243.3	351	21.9

2004 LEADERS

PASSING
Byron Leftwich
2,914 yards
15 TDs
60.5 comp
82.2 rating

RUSHING
Fred Taylor
1,224 yards

RECEIVING
Jimmy Smith
74 receptions
1,172 yards

TACKLES
Mike Peterson
93

SACKS
Greg Favors
John Henderson
5.5

INTERCEPTIONS
Donovin Darius
Rashean Mathis
5

BY THE NUMBERS:

7

The Jaguars had a flair for the dramatic in 2004. Eleven of their games were decided by seven points or less. And every one of those contests was decided on the final possession of the game.

JACKSONVILLE JAGUARS

2004 RECORD: 9–7

Head coach Jack Del Rio has made good on his promise to transform the Jaguars into one of the NFL's top defensive teams. Now it is time for the offense to shine. The spotlight, of course, falls on quarterback Byron Leftwich, the team's No. 1 draft pick in 2003. At 6-5, 245 pounds, Byron is the prototype for the new NFL quarterback: big, strong, and fast. So far, Byron has displayed maturity beyond his years. He was one of the league's top rookies in 2003 and improved in just about every area in 2004. Favorite targets Jimmy Smith and Reggie Williams both return, along with heavy-duty running back Fred Taylor. With so much experience and depth, anything less than a playoff appearance in 2005 will be a disappointment.

QUARTERBACK BYRON LEFTWICH IS ON THE VERGE OF SUPERSTARDOM. HE WILL TRY TO LEAD THE JAGUARS INTO POSTSEASON PLAY IN 2005.

Main: Scott Halleran. Inset: Scott Halleran.

2004 TEAM STATS

	RANK	YPG	RUSH YPG	PASS YPG	PTS	PTS/GAME
OFFENSE	21	313.1	115.6	197.4	261	16.3
DEFENSE	11	320.9	111.1	209.8	280	17.5

TENNESSEE TITANS

Okay, take it easy. There is no need to panic. Yes, the Titans had a disappointing year in 2004. When you win 12 games one season and then lose almost that many the next season, something obviously has gone wrong. Injuries to key personnel, including quarterback Steve McNair, played a major role in the Titans' slump. That's just bad luck. But there were bright spots, too, including the continued growth of Pro Bowl linebacker Keith Bulluck. Here's the bottom line: head coach Jeff Fisher has made Tennessee one of the NFL's most successful franchises. One bad season is not the end of the world. The Titans will be back.

AFC SOUTH

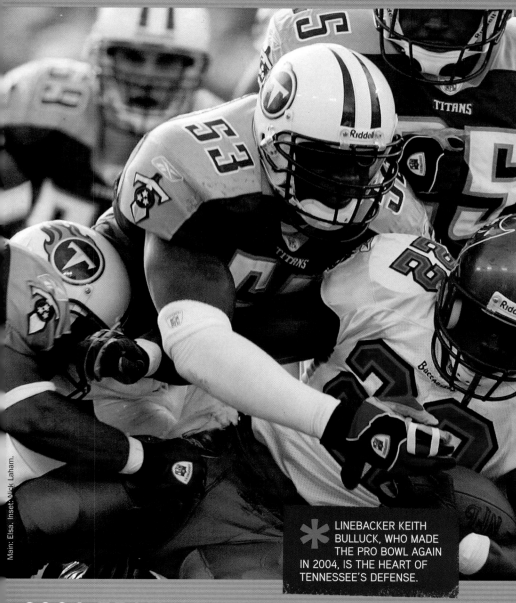

Main: Elsa. Inset: Nick Laham.

* LINEBACKER KEITH BULLUCK, WHO MADE THE PRO BOWL AGAIN IN 2004, IS THE HEART OF TENNESSEE'S DEFENSE.

2004 LEADERS

PASSING
Billy Volek
2,486 yards
18 TDs
61.1 comp
87.1 rating

RUSHING
Chris Brown
1,067 yards

RECEIVING
Drew Bennett
80 receptions
1,247 yards

TACKLES
Keith Bulluck
100

SACKS
Kevin Carter
6.0

INTERCEPTIONS
Andre Dyson
6

BY THE NUMBERS:

1,247

That is the total receiving yardage for Drew Bennett, who had the best season of his career.

2004 TEAM STATS

	RANK	YPG	RUSH YPG	PASS YPG	PTS	PTS/GAME
OFFENSE	11	342.9	116.9	226.0	344	21.5
DEFENSE	27	357.8	119.8	237.9	439	27.4

2004 LEADERS

PASSING
Kyle Boller
2,559 yards
13 TDs
55.6 comp
70.9 rating

RUSHING
Jamal Lewis
1,006 yards

RECEIVING
Travis Taylor
34 receptions
421 yards

TACKLES
Ray Lewis
100

SACKS
Terrell Suggs
10.5

INTERCEPTIONS
Ed Reed
9

BY THE NUMBERS:

7

That is how many times linebacker Ray Lewis has been selected to play in the Pro Bowl.

BALTIMORE RAVENS
2004 RECORD: 9–7

After a somewhat disappointing season in which they barely cracked the .500 barrier, the Ravens have more questions than answers in 2005. But few problems will be found on the defensive side of the ball. Defense is a Baltimore trademark, and that won't change this season, not with 2004's Defensive Player of the Year Ed Reed at safety. Ed emerged from the long shadow of teammate Ray Lewis in 2004 and helped the Ravens maintain their reputation as one of the NFL's toughest defensive units. With the speed of a world-class sprinter and a knack for snatching the ball away from receivers, Ed is the best defensive back in the game. In fact, he's the first safety in two decades to be named the league's top defensive player. With a little help from the offense, the Ravens could be contenders in 2005.

✱ ALL-PRO SAFETY ED REED HAD A LEAGUE-HIGH NINE INTERCEPTIONS IN 2004. HE ALSO SET AN NFL RECORD BY RETURNING ONE OF THOSE INTERCEPTIONS 106 YARDS FOR A TOUCHDOWN.

Main: Doug Pensinger. Inset: Doug Pensinger.

2004 TEAM STATS

	RANK	YPG	RUSH YPG	PASS YPG	PTS	PTS/GAME
OFFENSE	31	273.4	128.9	144.5	317	19.8
DEFENSE	6	300.2	105.1	195.1	268	16.8

CINCINNATI
BENGALS

2004 RECORD: 8-8

No one ever said it was easy trying to live up to great expectations. Just ask quarterback Carson Palmer, who arrived in Cincinnati carrying a Heisman Trophy and the hopes of a franchise. The top pick in the 2003 NFL Draft, Carson finally stepped into a starting role in 2004. While there were undeniable growing pains, there were also signs that Carson is ready to lead Cincinnati to new heights. After a slow start in 2004, the Bengals won seven of their last eleven games. With a year of experience under his belt, Carson should be even better in 2005. And that could signal a playoff run for the Bengals.

Main: Ezra Shaw. Inset: Doug Pensinger.

* IN HIS FIRST YEAR AS A STARTER, QB CARSON PALMER IMPROVED DRAMATICALLY AS THE SEASON WORE ON. A SURE SIGN OF MATURITY: CARSON WAS AT HIS BEST IN CLOSE GAMES. HE'S A CLUTCH PLAYER.

2004 LEADERS

PASSING
Carson Palmer
2,897 yards
18 TDs
60.9 comp
77.3 rating

RUSHING
Rudi Johnson
1,454 yards

RECEIVING
Chad Johnson
95 receptions
1,274 yards

TACKLES
Brian Simmons
73

SACKS
Justin Smith
8.0

INTERCEPTIONS
Tory James
8

BY THE NUMBERS:
497

That is the increase in rushing yardage for Rudi Johnson from 2003 to 2004. The sturdy (5-10, 233) running back started every game and set Bengals single-season records for rushing yards (1,454) and carries (361). He also scored a team-high twelve touchdowns.

2004 TEAM STATS

	RANK	YPG	RUSH YPG	PASS YPG	PTS	PTS/GAME
OFFENSE	18	321.3	114.9	206.3	374	23.4
DEFENSE	19	335.3	128.9	206.4	372	23.3

CLEVELAND
BROWNS

2004 RECORD: **4–12**

It isn't often that the arrival of a new coach steals all the headlines. But that's what happened in Cleveland last winter when Romeo Crennel agreed to take on the job of rebuilding one of the league's oldest and proudest franchises. There is a lot of work to be done in Cleveland. The Browns have won a total of only nine games in the past two seasons. But if anyone is up to the task, it is Crennel, the former defensive coordinator of the New England Patriots. Romeo brings a wealth of experience to his new position, as well as five Super Bowl rings! The Browns will have a lot of new faces in the lineup in 2005, and you can be sure of one thing: they will play as hard as any team in the league. With Romeo Crennel in charge, it should not be long before the Browns turn things around.

AFC NORTH

2004 LEADERS

PASSING
Jeff Garcia
1,731 yards
10 TDs
57.1 comp
76.7 rating

RUSHING
Lee Suggs
744 yards

RECEIVING
Dennis Northcutt
55 receptions
806 yards

TACKLES
Robert Griffith
92

SACKS
Ebenezer Ekuban
8.0

INTERCEPTIONS
Anthony Henry
4

BY THE NUMBERS:

5

That's the number of Super Bowl rings owned by new head coach Romeo Crennel. He won three as defensive coordinator of the New England Patriots and two more when he was an assistant with the New York Giants under Bill Parcells.

* CORNERBACK DAYLON McCUTCHEON WAS ONE OF THE BRIGHT SPOTS FOR A CLEVELAND DEFENSE THAT SPENT A LOT OF TIME ON THE FIELD IN 2004.

Main: Tom Hauck. Inset: Brian Bahr.

2004 TEAM STATS

	RANK	YPG	RUSH YPG	PASS YPG	PTS	PTS/GAME
OFFENSE	28	280.1	103.6	176.5	276	17.3
DEFENSE	15	325.9	144.6	181.3	390	24.4

PITTSBURGH
STEELERS

2004 RECORD: **15–1**

Talk about a reversal of fortune! The Steelers won only six games in 2003 and split their first two games of the 2004 season. This appeared to be a team going nowhere fast. Then rookie quarterback Ben Roethlisberger stepped in for the injured Tommy Maddox, and suddenly the Steelers were on the most improbable roll in recent NFL memory. They were the hottest team in the league, reeling off 15 straight victories. The storybook season finally came to an end in the AFC Championship Game, with a loss to the mighty New England Patriots. Returning in 2005 are Big Ben and most of his supporting cast, including punishing running back Jerome Bettis and gifted wide receiver Hines Ward. Led by third-year strong safety Troy Polamalu, the Steelers also had the top-ranked defense in the NFL. With that kind of talent, they will not sneak up on anyone this year.

Main: Tom Pidgeon. Inset: Al Bello.

✱ WITH OUTSTANDING PASS COVERAGE AND 67 TACKLES, TROY POLAMALU HELPED THE STEELERS FINISH 2004 AS THE NFL'S BEST DEFENSE.

2004 LEADERS

PASSING
Ben Roethlisberger
2,621 yards
17 TDs
66.4 comp
98.1 rating

RUSHING
Jerome Bettis
941 yards

RECEIVING
Hines Ward
80 receptions
1,004 yards

TACKLES
Troy Polamalu
67

SACKS
Aaron Smith
8.0

INTERCEPTIONS
Troy Polamalu
5

BY THE NUMBERS:
98.1

That was Ben Roethlisberger's quarterback rating in 2004. That is the highest rating ever for a rookie. Quarterback is supposed to be a difficult position to learn in the NFL, but Ben made it look easy. Not surprisingly, he was named Offensive Rookie of the Year.

2004 TEAM STATS

	RANK	YPG	RUSH YPG	PASS YPG	PTS	PTS/GAME
OFFENSE	16	324.0	154.0	170.0	372	23.3
DEFENSE	1	258.4	81.2	177.2	251	15.7

15

2004 LEADERS

PASSING
Jake Plummer
4,089 yards
27 TDs
58.2 comp
84.5 rating

RUSHING
Reuben Droughns
1,240 yards

RECEIVING
Rod Smith
79 receptions
1,144 yards

TACKLES
D.J. Williams
81

SACKS
Reggie Hayward
10.5

INTERCEPTIONS
Champ Bailey
3

BY THE NUMBERS:

712

Career receptions for wide receiver Rod Smith, who has been the Broncos' top pass catcher for the past eight seasons. Now in his eleventh year in the NFL, Rod shows no signs of slowing down. He remains a favorite target of QB Jake Plummer.

DENVER
2004 RECORD: 10–6
BRONCOS

In each of the past two seasons, the Broncos have finished 10–6 and made the playoffs. Not bad at all. But if quarterback Jake Plummer has anything to say about it, the Broncos will be playing deep into the month of January in 2005. This is a team that seems poised to make a run at a championship, thanks mainly to the powerful right arm of its superstar QB. Jake joined Denver as a highly touted free agent in 2003. Since then, he has more than lived up to his billing. In 2004 Jake was tireless, taking every single snap from center. He set a franchise record for passing yards and tied the mark for touchdown passes in a season. But Jake is not interested in records. It is a Super Bowl ring he wants.

* THROWING LONG AND OFTEN, QUARTERBACK JAKE PLUMMER HAD HIS BEST SEASON AS A PRO IN 2004. HIS 4,089 YARDS PASSING WAS A DENVER RECORD.

Main: Stephen Dunn. Inset: Brian Bahr.

2004 TEAM STATS

	RANK	YPG	RUSH YPG	PASS YPG	PTS	PTS/GAME
OFFENSE	5	395.8	145.8	249.9	381	23.8
DEFENSE	4	278.7	94.5	184.2	304	19.0

KANSAS CITY CHIEFS

2004 RECORD: **7–9**

Putting points on the board will not be a problem in 2005 for the Chiefs, who led the NFL in total offense last year. Not when you have electrifying kickoff return specialist Dante Hall, whose 1,718 yards was tops in the NFL. Although at 5-8 he is one of the league's smallest players, no one can change the course of a game quite like Dante. He twice returned kickoffs for touchdowns in 2004, and had six returns of more than 40 yards. With Dante in uniform, the Chiefs are sure to get the ball in good field position. It is no wonder they score so many points. If the defense improves, the Chiefs should be playoff contenders.

2004 LEADERS

PASSING
Trent Green
4,591 yards
27 TDs
66.4 comp
95.2 rating

RUSHING
Priest Holmes
892 yards

RECEIVING
Tony Gonzalez
102 receptions
1,258 yards

TACKLES
Scott Fujita
67

SACKS
Jared Allen
9.0

INTERCEPTIONS
Eric Warfield
Greg Wesley
4

BY THE NUMBERS:

102

Number of receptions by tight end Tony Gonzalez in 2004. That mark not only led the league but was the most ever by a tight end in a season.

Main: Jonathan Daniel. Inset: Jeff Gross.

* DIMINUTIVE DANTE HALL IS ONE OF THE NFL'S MOST EXCITING PLAYERS. HE IS LISTED AS A WIDE RECEIVER, BUT IT IS ON SPECIAL TEAMS, RETURNING KICKOFFS, THAT DANTE HAS MADE HIS MARK.

2004 TEAM STATS

	RANK	YPG	RUSH YPG	PASS YPG	PTS	PTS/GAME
OFFENSE	1	418.4	143.1	275.4	483	30.2
DEFENSE	31	377.3	114.6	262.7	435	27.2

2004 LEADERS

PASSING
Kerry Collins
3,495 yards
21 TDs
56.3 comp
74.8 rating

RUSHING
Amos Zereoue
425 yards

RECEIVING
Jerry Porter
64 receptions
998 yards

TACKLES
Danny Clark
98

SACKS
Tommy Kelly
4.0

INTERCEPTIONS
Phillip Buchanon
3

BY THE NUMBERS:

90

In his seven seasons with the Vikings, new Raiders wide receiver Randy Moss already ranks sixth on the NFL's all-time list with 90 TD catches. Oakland fans hope he keeps up that incredible pace!

OAKLAND
RAIDERS

2004 RECORD: **5–11**

The Raiders acquired a lot of new players through trades, the draft, and free agency following a disappointing 2003 season. While progress was slow, the team did show improvement in 2004. The Raiders should only get better with the off-season acquisitions of Randy Moss and LaMont Jordan. In addition, the Raiders worked hard to sign potential free agent Jerry Porter to a long-term contract. A wide receiver with great hands and quick feet, Jerry teamed up with quarterback Kerry Collins to give the Raiders a potent aerial attack. Jerry finished the season with career highs in receptions (64), receiving yards (998), and touchdowns (9). A number of teams were interested in signing Jerry after that kind of performance, but the Raiders were not about to let him go. They figure an investment in Jerry is an investment in the future. And the future starts right now.

* THE RAIDERS CAN COUNT ON ANOTHER OUTSTANDING YEAR FROM WIDE RECEIVER JERRY PORTER—ESPECIALLY NOW THAT HE'LL BE JOINED BY ALL-PRO WR RANDY MOSS!

Main: Otto Greule, Jr. Inset: Tom Hauck.

2004 TEAM STATS

	RANK	YPG	RUSH YPG	PASS YPG	PTS	PTS/GAME
OFFENSE	17	322.1	80.9	241.1	320	20.0
DEFENSE	30	371.0	125.8	245.3	442	27.6

SAN DIEGO
CHARGERS

2004 RECORD: **12–4**

Wow! Talk about a surprise. In 2003 the Chargers were one of the NFL's lowliest teams, winning only four games and finishing at the bottom of the high-scoring AFC West. One year later they moved to the top of the standings with a 12–4 record. So what happened? A lot, actually. First of all, Drew Brees matured into one of the game's top quarterbacks and was named NFL Comeback Player of the Year. He finished third in the league with a 104.8 passer rating and was rewarded with a trip to the Pro Bowl. Brees was the leader of an explosive offense that scored 446 points, third most in team history. But he had help. Running back LaDainian Tomlinson had another solid year, as did tight end Antonio Gates. All are back in 2005, which could make the Chargers the best in the West. Again.

2004 LEADERS

PASSING
Drew Brees
3,159 yards
27 TDs
65.5 comp
104.8 rating

RUSHING
LaDainian Tomlinson
1,335 yards

RECEIVING
Antonio Gates
81 receptions
964 yards

TACKLES
Donnie Edwards
104

SACKS
Steve Foley
10.0

INTERCEPTIONS
Donnie Edwards
5

BY THE NUMBERS:
4.3

Since joining the Chargers in 2001, LaDainian Tomlinson has been one of the NFL's most consistent and productive running backs. He led the team in rushing again in 2004, and has a career average of 4.3 yards per carry.

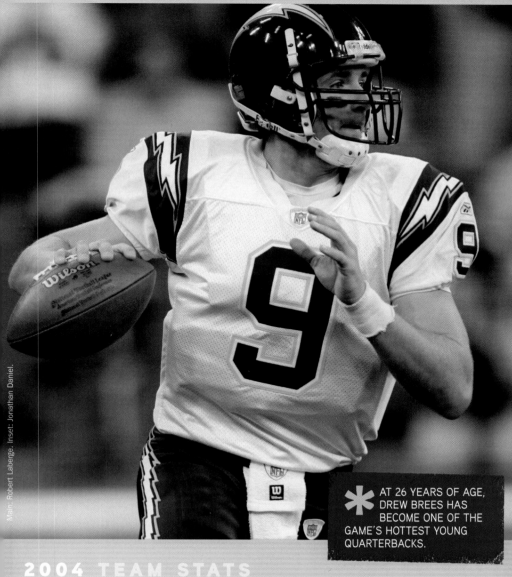

Main: Robert Laberge. Inset: Jonathan Daniel.

* AT 26 YEARS OF AGE, DREW BREES HAS BECOME ONE OF THE GAME'S HOTTEST YOUNG QUARTERBACKS.

2004 TEAM STATS

	RANK	YPG	RUSH YPG	PASS YPG	PTS	PTS/GAME
OFFENSE	10	346.4	136.6	209.8	446	27.9
DEFENSE	18	335.0	81.7	253.3	313	19.6

DALLAS
2004 RECORD: **6–10**
COWBOYS

The Cowboys were supposed to be Super Bowl contenders in 2004. Bill Parcells, one of the most successful coaches in NFL history, was in his second year. The pieces of the puzzle seemed to be falling into place after the team made the playoffs in 2003. Unfortunately, injuries and a sputtering offense slowed the Cowboys' return to greatness. But things are looking better for 2005. The Cowboys picked up veteran quarterback Drew Bledsoe in the offseason, which should stabilize the offense. Best of all, speedy running back Julius Jones, the team's leading rusher, has completely recovered from a broken shoulder blade. That spells trouble for the rest of the NFC.

2004 LEADERS

PASSING
Vinny Testaverde
3,532 yards
17 TDs
60.0 comp
76.4 rating

RUSHING
Julius Jones
819 yards

RECEIVING
Keyshawn Johnson
70 receptions
981 yards

TACKLES
Dat Nguyen
75

SACKS
Greg Ellis
9.0

INTERCEPTIONS
Terence Newman
4

BY THE NUMBERS:

39,808

Drew Bledsoe brings a wealth of experience to the Cowboys. The veteran quaterback has thrown for 39,808 yards in his career, which places him 10th on the NFL's all-time list. In Dallas he reunites with Bill Parcells, who coached Drew in New England.

* JULIUS JONES WAS THE COWBOYS' LEADING RUSHER IN 2004 DESPITE MISSING NEARLY HALF THE SEASON WITH AN INJURY. IMAGINE WHAT HE'LL BE LIKE WHEN HE'S HEALTHY.

Main: Jim McIsaac. Inset: Doug Pensinger.

2004 TEAM STATS

	RANK	YPG	RUSH YPG	PASS YPG	PTS	PTS/GAME
OFFENSE	14	324.8	110.6	214.3	293	18.3
DEFENSE	16	330.3	110.3	220.1	405	25.3

NEW YORK GIANTS

The waiting game is over. From this day forward, the New York Giants are Eli Manning's team. In 2004 Eli was a highly touted rookie out of the University of Mississippi. With a famous father (former All-Pro Archie Manning) and an MVP brother (Colts QB Peyton Manning), Eli naturally entered the league under a microscope. He did not have a lot of time to adjust. Head coach Tom Coughlin inserted Eli into the starting lineup midway through the season. Although he struggled at first, Eli eventually found his comfort zone. Veteran QB Kurt Warner is gone, so Eli will be the starter from day one in 2005. Jeremy Shockey is back at tight end, and leading rusher Tiki Barber also returns, giving the Giants a potent offense and legitimate playoff aspirations.

Main: Ezra Shaw. Inset: Ezra Shaw.

✱ THE GIANTS WILL BE EXPECTING BIG THINGS FROM SECOND-YEAR QUARTERBACK ELI MANNING, WHO DISPLAYED FLASHES OF BRILLIANCE AS A ROOKIE.

NFC EAST

2004 LEADERS

PASSING
Kurt Warner
2,054 yards
6 TDs
62.8 comp
86.5 rating

RUSHING
Tiki Barber
1,518 yards

RECEIVING
Amani Toomer
51 receptions
747 yards

TACKLES
Carlos Emmons
62

SACKS
Osi Umenyiora
7.0

INTERCEPTIONS
Brent Alexander
Gibril Wilson
3

BY THE NUMBERS:

118

The number of career sacks registered by six-time Pro Bowl defensive end Michael Strahan. Michael needs just 14 more sacks to catch Lawrence Taylor, the Giants' all-time leader.

2004 TEAM STATS

	RANK	YPG	RUSH YPG	PASS YPG	PTS	PTS/GAME
OFFENSE	23	295.1	119.0	176.1	303	18.9
DEFENSE	13	324.2	134.8	189.4	347	21.7

PHILADELPHIA EAGLES

2004 RECORD: **13–3**

After three straight appearances in the NFC Championship Game, the Eagles made a handful of strong player personnel moves prior to the 2004 season. They had only one goal: to win the Super Bowl. And they nearly pulled it off. The Eagles' magical season did not come to an end until Super Bowl XXXIX, in which they lost to the New England Patriots, 24–21. It was quite a ride for the Eagles and their fans. But don't be fooled into thinking this team is satisfied. The Eagles have some unfinished business. With a lineup that includes quarterback Donovan McNabb, running back Brian Westbrook, and wide receiver Terrell Owens, they might just make another Super Bowl appearance in 2005.

2004 LEADERS

PASSING
Donovan McNabb
3,875 yards
31 TDs
64.0 comp
104.7 rating

RUSHING
Brian Westbrook
812 yards

RECEIVING
Terrell Owens
77 receptions
1,200 yards

TACKLES
Michael Lewis
74

SACKS
Jevon Kearse
7.5

INTERCEPTIONS
Lito Sheppard
5

BY THE NUMBERS:

9

No one thought Terrell Owens would be able to play in Super Bowl XXXIX. After all, his broken ankle had been surgically repaired just six weeks earlier. Not only did "TO" play, he caught nine passes!

* THE VERSATILE DONOVAN McNABB RETURNS AT QUARTERBACK FOR THE NFC CHAMPION EAGLES.

Main: Andy Lyons. Inset: Greg Fiume.

2004 TEAM STATS

	RANK	YPG	RUSH YPG	PASS YPG	PTS	PTS/GAME
OFFENSE	9	351.1	102.4	248.7	386	24.1
DEFENSE	10	319.7	118.9	200.8	260	16.3

WASHINGTON
REDSKINS

2004 RECORD: **6–10**

You did not expect a man like Joe Gibbs to be happy with a losing season, did you? Gibbs, one of the NFL's most accomplished coaches, returned to the Washington sidelines in 2004. The Redskins struggled most of the year, especially on offense, so it is not surprising that a number of changes have been made. These include the acquisition of wide receivers Santana Moss from the New York Jets and David Patten from the New England Patriots, as well as center Casey Rabach of the Baltimore Ravens. Expect running back Clinton Portis to be the workhorse of the offense, as he was in 2004. There are no problems on defense—the Redskins held opponents to just 16.6 points a game and were ranked third in the NFL.

2004 LEADERS

PASSING
Patrick Ramsey
1,665 yards
10 TDs
62.1 comp
74.8 rating

RUSHING
Clinton Portis
1,315 yards

RECEIVING
Laveranues Coles
90 receptions
950 yards

TACKLES
Marcus Washington
87

SACKS
Cornelius Griffin
Shawn Springs
6.0

INTERCEPTIONS
Shawn Springs
5

Main: Jamie Squire. Inset: Jamie Squire.

* IN HIS FIRST YEAR IN A REDSKINS UNIFORM, CLINTON PORTIS WAS A BIG SUCCESS. HE RUSHED FOR A TEAM-HIGH 1,315 YARDS.

BY THE NUMBERS:
707,920

Regular-season home paid attendance for the Washington Redskins in 2004, the most in NFL history. Washington has led the NFL in regular-season home paid attendance in each of the past five seasons.

2004 TEAM STATS

	RANK	YPG	RUSH YPG	PASS YPG	PTS	PTS/GAME
OFFENSE	30	274.8	110.3	164.5	240	15.0
DEFENSE	3	267.6	81.5	186.1	265	16.6

NFC SOUTH

2004
LEADERS

PASSING
Michael Vick
2,313 yards
14 TDs
56.4 comp
78.1 rating

RUSHING
Warrick Dunn
1,106 yards

RECEIVING
Alge Crumpler
48 receptions
774 yards

TACKLES
Keith Brooking
86

SACKS
Patrick Kerney
13.0

INTERCEPTIONS
Aaron Beasley
4

BY THE NUMBERS:
559

That is the number of solo tackles accumulated by linebacker Keith Brooking in his eight-year career. Keith led the Falcons in that category again in 2004 and was named to the Pro Bowl for the fifth time.

ATLANTA
FALCONS

2004 RECORD: 11–5

If there is such a thing as a "franchise player," then quarterback Michael Vick is surely it. How much does Michael mean to the Falcons? Consider this: in 2003, with Michael sidelined by a broken leg, the team posted a 5–11 record. In 2004, with the electrifying Mr. Vick back in the lineup, the Falcons reversed those numbers and finished first in the NFC South. A brilliant all-around athlete who can beat you through the air or on the ground, Michael was named to his second Pro Bowl. It's no surprise that Atlanta offered him a long-term contract late in the season and made him one of the highest-paid players in history. It's only a matter of time before Michael leads the Falcons to the Super Bowl!

Main: Scott Halleran. Inset: Scott Halleran.

*** AT ONLY SIX FEET TALL, MICHAEL VICK IS NOT THE BIGGEST PLAYER IN THE LEAGUE. BUT THERE IS NO QUARTERBACK MORE EXCITING—OR MORE IMPORTANT TO HIS TEAM.

2004 TEAM STATS

	RANK	YPG	RUSH YPG	PASS YPG	PTS	PTS/GAME
OFFENSE	20	317.8	167.0	150.8	340	21.3
DEFENSE	14	325.4	105.1	220.4	337	21.1

CAROLINA
PANTHERS

2004 RECORD: **7–9**

Two years ago the Panthers were the Cinderella story of the NFL, posting one of the most dramatic turnarounds in league history. They went from 1–15 in 2001 to 7–9 in 2002. And then, in 2003, they made it all the way to the Super Bowl! Was Carolina suddenly a dynasty? Or a one-hit wonder? Well, the jury is still out on that one. Decimated by injuries, the Panthers lost seven of their first eight games in 2004 and failed to make the playoffs. But with quarterback Jake Delhomme continuing to improve, the Panthers should be back on the winning track in 2005. Delhomme had his finest season as a pro in 2004, throwing 29 touchdown passes. Seventeen of those came in the second half of the season, as the Panthers won six of their last eight games.

Main: Brian Bahr. Inset: Craig Jones.

* SINCE TAKING OVER AS CAROLINA'S STARTING QB MIDWAY THROUGH THE 2003 SEASON, JAKE DELHOMME HAS PROVED TO BE ONE OF THE NFL'S FINEST QUARTERBACKS.

NFC SOUTH

2004 LEADERS

PASSING
Jake Delhomme
3,886 yards
29 TDs
58.2 comp
87.3 rating

RUSHING
Nick Goings
821 yards

RECEIVING
Muhsin Muhammad
93 receptions
1,405 yards

TACKLES
Will Witherspoon
85

SACKS
Julius Peppers
11.0

INTERCEPTIONS
Chris Gamble
6

BY THE NUMBERS:
6-6, 285

Height and weight of Panthers defensive end Julius Peppers. Despite his size, Julius is one of the league's quickest players, and has amassed 30 sacks in three seasons. Julius played both basketball and football at the University of North Carolina.

2004 TEAM STATS

	RANK	YPG	RUSH YPG	PASS YPG	PTS	PTS/GAME
OFFENSE	13	326.6	98.9	227.7	355	22.2
DEFENSE	20	336.4	119.0	217.4	339	21.2

2004 LEADERS

PASSING
Aaron Brooks
3,810 yards
21 TDs
57.0 comp
79.5 rating

RUSHING
Deuce McAllister
1,074 yards

RECEIVING
Joe Horn
94 receptions
1,399 yards

TACKLES
Tebucky Jones
78

SACKS
Darren Howard
11.0

INTERCEPTIONS
Mike McKenzie
5

BY THE NUMBERS:

64

Safety Jay Bellamy anchors the Saints' defense. He has also started every game since coming to New Orleans four years ago. That is 64 consecutive regular-season games.

NEW ORLEANS
SAINTS
2004 RECORD: **8–8**

Talk about a roller-coaster ride. The Saints slipped to 4–8 in 2004 before rallying to win their last four games; they nearly made the playoffs. Scoring points should not be a problem in 2005 thanks to players like quarterback Aaron Brooks, running back Deuce McAllister, and, especially, wide receiver Joe Horn. At 32, Joe made the Pro Bowl and had the best season of his career. He caught 94 passes and equaled or broke team records for receiving yards and touchdowns. At an age when many players are thinking about retirement, Joe Horn is just hitting his stride! With a little improvement on the defensive side of the ball, the Saints will be a team to watch in 2005.

Main: Chris Graythen. Inset: Matthew Stockman.

✳ EXPECT THE SAINTS TO PUT A LOT OF POINTS ON THE SCOREBOARD IN 2005, THANKS TO PLAYERS LIKE JOE HORN, ONE OF THE NFL'S TOP RECEIVERS.

2004 TEAM STATS

	RANK	YPG	RUSH YPG	PASS YPG	PTS	PTS/GAME
OFFENSE	15	324.6	100.4	224.2	348	21.8
DEFENSE	32	383.8	140.8	243.0	405	25.3

TAMPA BAY
BUCCANEERS
2004 RECORD: **5–11**

In 2004, the Bucs had the NFL's fifth-ranked defense. The heart and soul of that unit, as usual, was linebacker Derrick Brooks. After logging a team-high 109 tackles, Derrick was named to his eighth straight Pro Bowl. He is one of five players in NFL history who have earned eight Pro Bowl berths, won a Super Bowl, and been named NFL Defensive Player of the Year. The others are Jack Lambert, Mike Singletary, Lawrence Taylor, and Reggie White. That's pretty impressive company. Derrick is also a true iron man: he has not missed a single game in his 10-year career. And he doesn't plan on missing any this year. In fact, if Derrick has his way, he will be on the field in January—in the playoffs!

2004 LEADERS

PASSING
Brian Griese
2,632 yards
20 TDs
69.3 comp
97.5 rating

RUSHING
Michael Pittman
926 yards

RECEIVING
Michael Clayton
80 receptions
1,193 yards

TACKLES
Derrick Brooks
109

SACKS
Simeon Rice
12.0

INTERCEPTIONS
Brian Kelly
4

BY THE NUMBERS:

105

Defensive end Simeon Rice has been a quarterback's worst nightmare since he entered the league nine years ago. Simeon led the Bucs in sacks in 2004 with 12, bringing his career total to 105.

* HOW DO YOU STOP LINE-BACKER DERRICK BROOKS? GOOD QUESTION. OPPONENTS HAVE BEEN TRYING FOR TEN YEARS, AND NO ONE HAS HAD MUCH LUCK.

Main: Doug Pensinger. Inset: Andy Lyons.

2004 TEAM STATS

	RANK	YPG	RUSH YPG	PASS YPG	PTS	PTS/GAME
OFFENSE	22	310.2	93.1	217.1	301	18.8
DEFENSE	5	284.5	123.3	161.2	304	19.0

2004 LEADERS

PASSING
Chad Hutchinson
903 yards
4 TDs
57.1 comp
73.6 rating

RUSHING
Thomas Jones
948 yards

RECEIVING
David Terrell
42 receptions
699 yards

TACKLES
Lance Briggs
102

SACKS
Alex Brown
6.0

INTERCEPTIONS
Nathan Vasher
5

BY THE NUMBERS:

144

Linebacker Brian Urlacher, a three-time Pro Bowler, is the emotional leader of the Chicago defense. Although he's only been in the league four years, Brian is the Bears' career leader in fumble recovery yardage with 144 yards.

CHICAGO
2004 RECORD: **5–11**
BEARS

Head Coach Lovie Smith will enter the 2005 season with a new offensive weapon, as the Bears signed free agent wide receiver Muhsin Muhammad from the Carolina Panthers. Muhsin should have an immediate impact in Chicago. At 31 years of age he had the best season of his career in 2004, catching 93 passes for a league-high 1,405 yards. He also scored 16 touchdowns. Muhsin gives the Bears instant credibility on offense. With great hands and exceptional speed, he is the kind of player who can change the course of a game in a heartbeat. Obviously Muhsin cannot carry the Bears to the playoffs by himself. But his arrival is a big step in the right direction.

Main: Scott Halleran. Inset: Al Bello.

* ADEWALE OGUNLEYE LED THE AFC IN SACKS WHILE PLAYING WITH MIAMI IN 2003.

2004 TEAM STATS

	RANK	YPG	RUSH YPG	PASS YPG	PTS	PTS/GAME
OFFENSE	32	238.5	101.5	137.0	231	14.4
DEFENSE	21	336.9	128.1	208.8	331	20.7

DETROIT
LIONS

2004 RECORD: **6–10**

You have to walk before you can run. The Detroit Lions are now two years into a massive rebuilding project led by head coach Steve Mariucci. And while the record may not show it yet, the Lions are definitely an improved team. You want proof? Look no further than wide receiver Roy Williams, a first-round draft pick in 2004. With spectacular leaping ability and a knack for making acrobatic catches look easy, Roy has almost single-handedly brought excitement back to the game of football in the Motor City. With 54 receptions, Roy not only led the Lions in receptions, he also set a team rookie record. Keep an eye on Roy this season—and on the Lions. They're a team to watch.

2004 LEADERS

PASSING
Joey Harrington
3,047 yards
19 TDs
56.0 comp
77.5 rating

RUSHING
Kevin Jones
1,133 yards

RECEIVING
Roy Williams
54 receptions
817 yards

TACKLES
Earl Holmes
78

SACKS
James Hall
11.5

INTERCEPTIONS
Dre' Bly
4

*IN JUST ONE SEASON WIDE RECEIVER ROY WILLIAMS HAS EARNED THE RESPECT OF OPPONENTS AND THE ADMIRATION OF HIS TEAMMATES.

Miami: Jonathan Daniel. Inset: Tom Pidgeon.

BY THE NUMBERS:

3,047

Passing yards by quarter-back Joey Harrington, who continued his steady improvement in 2004. Joey is only the third QB in Lions history to surpass the 3,000-yard mark in a season.

2004 TEAM STATS

	RANK	YPG	RUSH YPG	PASS YPG	PTS	PTS/GAME
OFFENSE	24	293.3	111.1	182.3	296	18.5
DEFENSE	22	337.6	117.9	219.6	350	21.9

GREEN BAY
PACKERS

2004 RECORD: **10–6**

No pain, no gain. If you want something, you have to be willing to work for it. Just ask Javon Walker. After two seasons in the NFL, the Packers' gifted wide receiver decided he wanted to be one of the league's best players. So he worked ferociously in the offseason. He added muscle to his frame and ran sprints in the Arizona desert until he felt like his legs were going to fall off. The result? In 2004 Javon became the favorite target of Packers quarterback Brett Favre. He caught a team-high 89 passes and scored 12 touchdowns as Green Bay posted its fifth straight winning season. Expect the Favre-Walker combination, and the Packers, to be even better this year.

2004 LEADERS

PASSING
Brett Favre
4,088 yards
30 TDs
64.1 comp
92.4 rating

RUSHING
Ahman Green
1,163 yards

RECEIVING
Javon Walker
89 receptions
1,382 yards

TACKLES
Nick Barnett
92

SACKS
Kabeer Gbaja-Biamila
13.5

INTERCEPTIONS
Darren Sharper
4

BY THE NUMBERS:

189

You would have to look long and hard to find a tougher player than Green Bay quarterback Brett Favre. The Packers superstar has started 189 consecutive regular-season games.

* NOW IN HIS FOURTH SEASON, WIDE RECEIVER JAVON WALKER HAS EMERGED AS AN ALL-PRO CANDIDATE FOR THE PACKERS.

Main: Jonathan Daniel; Insert: Brian Bahr.

2004 TEAM STATS

	RANK	YPG	RUSH YPG	PASS YPG	PTS	PTS/GAME
OFFENSE	3	397.3	119.3	278.1	424	26.5
DEFENSE	25	346.3	117.4	228.9	380	23.8

MINNESOTA VIKINGS

2004 RECORD: **8–8**

If you are going to build a franchise around a single player, there are not many better choices than Vikings quarterback Daunte Culpepper. Now entering his seventh season, Daunte seems poised to become the NFL's premier signal caller. He came close in 2004, posting MVP-caliber numbers and earning a spot in the Pro Bowl. What makes Daunte so good? Well, at 6-4, 264 pounds, he's bigger than most linebackers. He can throw the ball 60 yards downfield, on a rope, and he can run like a fullback. Granted, the departure of wide receiver Randy Moss leaves Daunte without his favorite target, but that obstacle can be overcome. The Vikings made the playoffs in 2004. They should return in 2005.

Main: Brian Bahr. Inset: Andy Lyons.

* THERE IS ALMOST NO STOPPING QUARTERBACK DAUNTE CULPEPPER, WHO COULD BE THE LEAGUE'S MVP IN 2005.

2004 LEADERS

PASSING
Daunte Culpepper
4,717 yards
39 TDs
69.2 comp
110.9 rating

RUSHING
Onterrio Smith
544 yards

RECEIVING
Nate Burleson
68 receptions
1,006 yards

TACKLES
E.J. Henderson
65

SACKS
Kevin Williams
11.5

INTERCEPTIONS
Antoine Winfield
3

BY THE NUMBERS:

311

How would you like to line up against defensive tackle Kevin Williams, who weighs 311 pounds? Most teams have all kinds of trouble stopping Kevin, who has led the Vikings in sacks in each of his two seasons in the NFL.

2004 TEAM STATS

	RANK	YPG	RUSH YPG	PASS YPG	PTS	PTS/GAME
OFFENSE	4	396.2	113.9	282.3	405	25.3
DEFENSE	28	368.9	125.4	243.5	395	24.7

2004 LEADERS

PASSING
Josh McCown
2,511 yards
11 TDs
57.1 comp
74.1 rating

RUSHING
Emmitt Smith
937 yards

RECEIVING
Larry Fitzgerald
58 receptions
780 yards

TACKLES
Adrian Wilson
80

SACKS
Bertrand Berry
14.5

INTERCEPTIONS
David Macklin
4

BY THE NUMBERS:

107-80

That is the career mark of head coach Dennis Green, who begins his second season in Arizona. Green brings a long track record of success, having led the Minnesota Vikings to eight postseason appearances.

ARIZONA
2004 RECORD: 6–10
CARDINALS

The transition began in 2004, as the rebuilding Cardinals struggled to adjust to a new head coach, a new system, and a number of new faces. But there was improvement: after winning only four games in 2003, the Cards went 6–10 a year ago, giving fans hope that first-year head coach Dennis Green has the team moving upward. Defense was the name of the game for the Cardinals, thanks mainly to the marauding play of defensive end Bertrand Berry. Signed as a free agent in the spring of 2004, Bertrand stepped right in and became an instant force, leading the Cardinals in quarterback sacks. Time will tell, of course, but with Bertrand anchoring the defense, and Dennis Green at the helm, the Cardinals are prepared to take flight.

* THERE IS NOT A QUARTERBACK IN THE NFL WHO WANTS TO SEE ARIZONA DEFENSIVE END BERTRAND BERRY COMING AT HIM. BERTRAND IS ONE OF THE LEAGUE'S PREMIER PASS RUSHERS.

Main: Harry How. Inset: Otto Greule, Jr.

2004 TEAM STATS

	RANK	YPG	RUSH YPG	PASS YPG	PTS	PTS/GAME
OFFENSE	27	284.4	104.3	180.1	284	17.8
DEFENSE	12	321.3	131.6	189.8	322	20.1

ST. LOUIS
RAMS

Expectations were high for quarterback Marc Bulger and his St. Louis Rams in 2004. And why not? Shortly after leading the Rams to a 12–4 record, Marc was named MVP of the Pro Bowl. This was a team thinking "Super Bowl." But it did not quite work out that way. As the Rams advanced to the postseason but lost in the divisional round, Marc was a model of consistency, putting up the best numbers of his career. Pro Bowler Torry Holt was Marc's favorite target as the Rams fielded the league's sixth-best offense. Both players return in 2005. With some improvement on defense, the Rams should be contenders in the NFC West.

Main: Elsa. Inset: Jed Jacobsohn.

✳ MARC BULGER IS A SMART, EFFICIENT QUARTERBACK. HE THREW 21 TOUCHDOWNS PASSES IN 2004 AND WAS INTERCEPTED ONLY 14 TIMES.

NFC WEST

2004 LEADERS

PASSING
Marc Bulger
3,964 yards
21 TDs
66.2 comp
93.7 rating

RUSHING
Marshall Faulk
774 yards

RECEIVING
Torry Holt
94 receptions
1,372 yards

TACKLES
Pisa Tinoisamoa
76

SACKS
Bryce Fisher
8.5

INTERCEPTIONS
Jerametrius Butler
5

BY THE NUMBERS:

687

That is the number of career tackles made by linebacker Dexter Coakley, who joins the Rams as a free agent after spending eight years with the Dallas Cowboys. Dexter has also played in three Pro Bowls.

2004 TEAM STATS

	RANK	YPG	RUSH YPG	PASS YPG	PTS	PTS/GAME
OFFENSE	6	367.3	101.5	265.8	319	19.9
DEFENSE	17	334.6	136.2	198.4	392	24.5

SAN FRANCISCO 49ERS

2004 RECORD: 2–14

After one of the most challenging seasons in franchise history, the 49ers look for a fresh start in 2005. Enter Mike Nolan, who replaces head coach Dennis Erickson. Nolan was the defensive coordinator of the Baltimore Ravens, so it is no shock that one of his first goals will be to improve the 49ers' defense, which finished 24th in the NFL in 2004. That task will be made easier with the return of linebacker Julian Peterson, who was on his way to a third consecutive Pro Bowl season when he went down with an injury. Also back are safety Tony Parrish and linebacker Jeff Ulbrich. Expect major changes in the offense, which averaged only 16.2 points per game.

2004 LEADERS

PASSING
Tim Rattay
2,169 yards
10 TDs
60.9 comp
78.1 rating

RUSHING
Kevan Barlow
822 yards

RECEIVING
Eric Johnson
82 receptions
825 yards

TACKLES
Derek M. Smith
80

SACKS
John Engelberger
6.0

INTERCEPTIONS
Tony Parrish
4

BY THE NUMBERS:

5

No NFL franchise has been more successful than the 49ers in postseason play. They are one of only two teams in league history to win five Super Bowl titles.

SAFETY TONY PARRISH WAS A STANDOUT IN THE 49ERS SECONDARY WITH A TEAM-HIGH FOUR INTERCEPTIONS.

Main: Otto Greule, Jr. Inset: Jed Jacobsohn.

2004 TEAM STATS

	RANK	YPG	RUSH YPG	PASS YPG	PTS	PTS/GAME
OFFENSE	26	286.6	90.6	196.0	259	16.2
DEFENSE	24	342.6	124.7	217.9	452	28.3

SEATTLE SEAHAWKS

The Seattle Seahawks look to improve on last season's performance, when the club finished 9-7 and won the NFC West Division. The offense was steady, and should be strong again in 2005 thanks to the return of quarterback Matt Hasselbeck, wide receiver Darrell Jackson, and, especially, running back Shaun Alexander. Shaun, a 5-11, 225-pound sparkplug, was one of the NFL's best players in 2004, rushing for a team-record 1,696 yards and 20 touchdowns. Only Curtis Martin of the New York Jets gained more yards.

NFC WEST

2004 LEADERS

PASSING
Matt Hasselbeck
3,382 yards
22 TDs
58.9 comp
83.1 rating

RUSHING
Shaun Alexander
1,696 yards

RECEIVING
Darrell Jackson
87 receptions
1,199 yards

TACKLES
Marcus Trufant
86

SACKS
Chike Okeafor
8.5

INTERCEPTIONS
Ken Lucas
6

Main: Otto Greule, Jr. Inset: Chris Trotman.

* RUNNING BACK SHAUN ALEXANDER, WHO NEARLY WON THE NFL'S RUSHING TITLE IN 2004, WILL BE THE FOCUS OF THE SEAHAWKS' OFFENSE.

BY THE NUMBERS:

23.2

The Seahawks averaged 23.2 points per game in 2004 and were No. 8 among the NFL's 32 teams. With several talented, young players at skill positions, they could be ranked even higher in 2005.

2004 TEAM STATS

	RANK	YPG	RUSH YPG	PASS YPG	PTS	PTS/GAME
OFFENSE	8	352.1	130.9	221.2	371	23.2
DEFENSE	26	351.3	126.9	224.4	373	23.3

2001

AMERICAN CONFERENCE

Eastern Division	W	L	T	PTS	OP
New England	11	5	0	371	272
Miami	11	5	0	344	290
N.Y. Jets	10	6	0	308	295
Indianapolis	6	10	0	413	486
Buffalo	3	13	0	265	420

Central Division	W	L	T	PTS	OP
Pittsburgh	13	3	0	352	212
Baltimore	10	6	0	303	265
Cleveland	7	9	0	285	319
Tennessee	7	9	0	336	388
Jacksonville	6	10	0	294	286
Cincinnati	6	10	0	226	309

Western Division	W	L	T	PTS	OP
Oakland	10	6	0	399	327
Seattle	9	7	0	301	324
Denver	8	8	0	340	339
Kansas City	6	10	0	320	344
San Diego	5	11	0	332	321

NATIONAL CONFERENCE

Eastern Division	W	L	T	PTS	OP
Philadelphia	11	5	0	343	208
Washington	8	8	0	256	303
N.Y. Giants	7	9	0	294	321
Arizona	7	9	0	295	343
Dallas	5	11	0	246	338

Central Division	W	L	T	PTS	OP
Chicago	13	3	0	338	203
Green Bay	12	4	0	390	266
Tampa Bay	9	7	0	324	280
Minnesota	5	11	0	290	390
Detroit	2	14	0	270	424

Western Division	W	L	T	PTS	OP
St. Louis	14	2	0	503	273
San Francisco	12	4	0	409	282
New Orleans	7	9	0	333	409
Atlanta	7	9	0	291	377
Carolina	1	15	0	253	410

SUPER BOWL XXXVI
NEW ENGLAND 20, ST. LOUIS 17

MVP: QB TOM BRADY, NEW ENGLAND

Brian Bahr

SUPER BOWL XXXVII
TAMPA BAY 48, OAKLAND 21

MVP: FS DEXTER JACKSON, TAMPA BAY

2002

AMERICAN CONFERENCE

East	W	L	T	PTS.	OP
N.Y. Jets	9	7	0	359	336
New England	9	7	0	381	346
Miami	9	7	0	378	301
Buffalo	8	8	0	379	397

South	W	L	T	PTS.	OP
Tennessee	11	5	0	367	324
Indianapolis	10	6	0	349	313
Jacksonville	6	10	0	328	315
Houston	4	12	0	213	356

North	W	L	T	PTS.	OP
Pittsburgh	10	5	1	390	345
Cleveland	9	7	0	344	320
Baltimore	7	9	0	316	354
Cincinnati	2	14	0	279	456

West	W	L	T	PTS.	OP
Oakland	11	5	0	450	304
Denver	9	7	0	392	344
San Diego	8	8	0	333	367
Kansas City	8	8	0	467	399

NATIONAL CONFERENCE

East	W	L	T	PTS.	OP
Philadelphia	12	4	0	415	241
N.Y. Giants	10	6	0	320	279
Washington	7	9	0	307	365
Dallas	5	11	0	217	329

South	W	L	T	PTS.	OP
Tampa Bay	12	4	0	346	196
Atlanta	9	6	1	402	314
New Orleans	9	7	0	432	388
Carolina	7	9	0	258	302

North	W	L	T	PTS.	OP
Green Bay	12	4	0	398	328
Minnesota	6	10	0	390	442
Chicago	4	12	0	281	379
Detroit	3	13	0	306	451

West	W	L	T	PTS.	OP
San Francisco	10	6	0	367	351
Seattle	7	9	0	355	369
St. Louis	7	9	0	316	369
Arizona	5	11	0	262	417

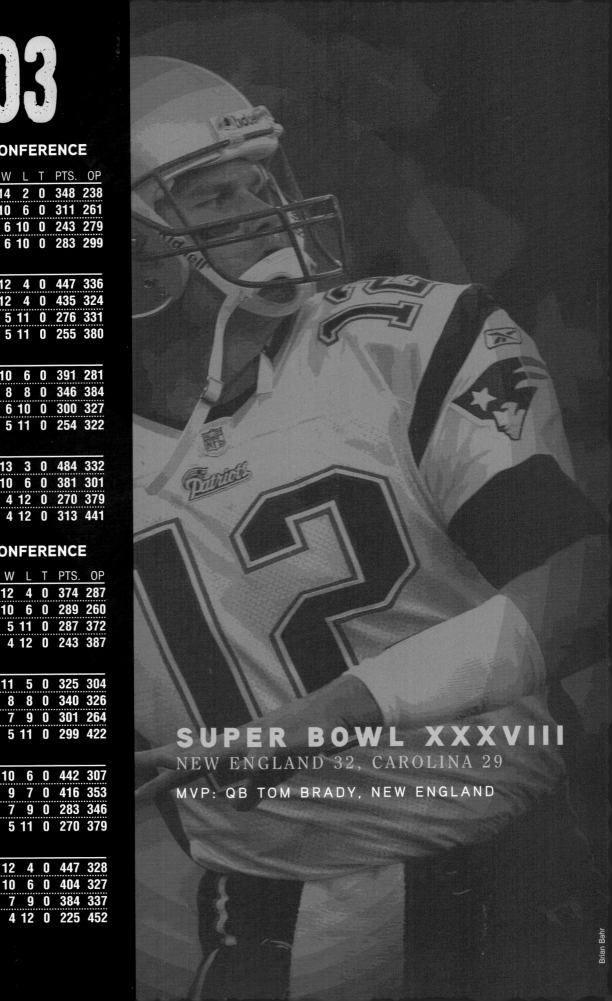

AMERICAN CONFERENCE

East

	W	L	T	PTS.	OP
New England	14	2	0	348	238
Miami	10	6	0	311	261
Buffalo	6	10	0	243	279
N.Y. Jets	6	10	0	283	299

South

	W	L	T	PTS.	OP
Indianapolis	12	4	0	447	336
Tennessee	12	4	0	435	324
Jacksonville	5	11	0	276	331
Houston	5	11	0	255	380

North

	W	L	T	PTS.	OP
Baltimore	10	6	0	391	281
Cincinnati	8	8	0	346	384
Pittsburgh	6	10	0	300	327
Cleveland	5	11	0	254	322

West

	W	L	T	PTS.	OP
Kansas City	13	3	0	484	332
Denver	10	6	0	381	301
Oakland	4	12	0	270	379
San Diego	4	12	0	313	441

NATIONAL CONFERENCE

East

	W	L	T	PTS.	OP
Philadelphia	12	4	0	374	287
Dallas	10	6	0	289	260
Washington	5	11	0	287	372
N.Y. Giants	4	12	0	243	387

South

	W	L	T	PTS.	OP
Carolina	11	5	0	325	304
New Orleans	8	8	0	340	326
Tampa Bay	7	9	0	301	264
Atlanta	5	11	0	299	422

North

	W	L	T	PTS.	OP
Green Bay	10	6	0	442	307
Minnesota	9	7	0	416	353
Chicago	7	9	0	283	346
Detroit	5	11	0	270	379

West

	W	L	T	PTS.	OP
St. Louis	12	4	0	447	328
Seattle	10	6	0	404	327
San Francisco	7	9	0	384	337
Arizona	4	12	0	225	452

SUPER BOWL XXXVIII
NEW ENGLAND 32, CAROLINA 29
MVP: QB TOM BRADY, NEW ENGLAND

Brian Bahr

AMERICAN CONFERENCE

East	W	L	T	PTS.	OP
New England	14	2	0	437	260
N.Y. Jets	10	6	0	333	261
Buffalo	9	7	0	395	284
Miami	4	12	0	275	354

South					
Indianapolis	12	4	0	522	313
Jacksonville	9	7	0	261	304
Houston	7	9	0	309	339
Tennessee	5	11	0	344	439

North					
Pittsburgh	15	1	0	372	251
Baltimore	9	7	0	317	268
Cincinnati	8	8	0	374	372
Cleveland	4	12	0	276	390

West					
San Diego	12	4	0	446	313
Denver	10	6	0	381	304
Kansas City	7	9	0	483	435
Oakland	5	11	0	320	442

NATIONAL CONFERENCE

East	W	L	T	PTS.	OP
Philadelphia	13	3	0	386	260
N.Y. Giants	6	10	0	303	347
Dallas	6	10	0	293	405
Washington	6	10	0	240	265

South					
Atlanta	11	5	0	340	337
New Orleans	8	8	0	348	405
Carolina	7	9	0	355	339
Tampa Bay	5	11	0	301	304

North					
Green Bay	10	6	0	424	380
Minnesota	8	8	0	405	395
Detroit	6	10	0	296	350
Chicago	5	11	0	231	331

West					
Seattle	9	7	0	371	373
St. Louis	8	8	0	319	392
Arizona	6	10	0	284	322
San Francisco	2	14	0	259	452

SUPER BOWL XXXIX
NEW ENGLAND 24, PHILADELPHIA 21

MVP: WR DEION BRANCH, NEW ENGLAND

Andy Lyons

TRACK THE TEAMS ON THE ROAD TO SUPER BOWL XL!

GET REALLY INVOLVED WITH THE NFL THIS YEAR—

week by week, all the way to the Super Bowl—thanks to your offical NFL Team Tracker. After each week's results, simply use your marker to record the standings on the standings chart (opposite page). Watch the games on television, read about them in newspapers, or get up-to-the-minute info at NFL.com. After each week, wipe off the old result and write in the latest win-loss records. When the playoffs begin, open the gatefold back cover to find your NFL Playoffs tracking grid. Keep track of the results as the teams strive to reach the ultimate goal— winning Super Bowl XL!

Jeff Gross.